Recent Ziggy Books

Ziggy in the Fast Lane

Ziggy's Follies

Ziggy's School of Hard Knocks

Ziggy on the Outside Looking In . . .

Look Out World . . . Here I Come!

Ziggy . . . A Rumor in His Own Time

A Day in the Life of Ziggy . . .

1-800-Ziggy

My Life as a Cartoon

Treasuries

Ziggy's Star Performances

The First 25 Years Are the Hardest!

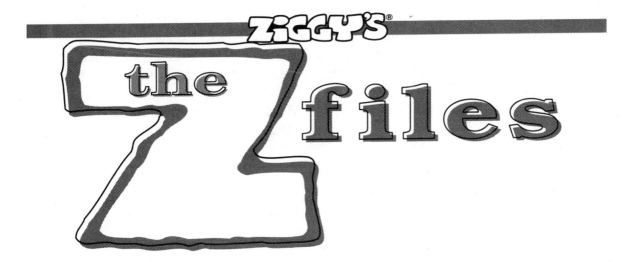

ZiGGY'S the Z files

BY Tom Wilson

**Andrews McMeel
Publishing**

Kansas City

www.uexpress.com and www.andrewsmcmeel.com

ISBN: 0-8362-3681-5

Library of Congress Catalog Card Number: 97-71638

98 99 00 01 BAH 10 9 8 7 6 5 4 3 2

─────ATTENTION: SCHOOLS AND BUSINESSES ─────

Andrews McMeel books are available at quantity discounts with bulk purchase for educational, business, or sales promotional use. For information, please write to: Special Sales Department, Andrews McMeel Publishing, 4520 Main Street, Kansas City, Missouri 64111.

13

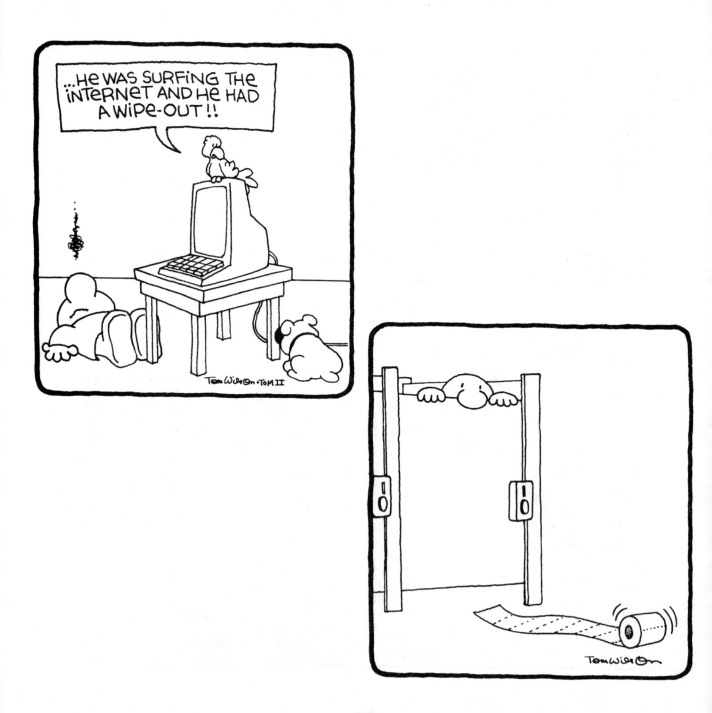

52

64

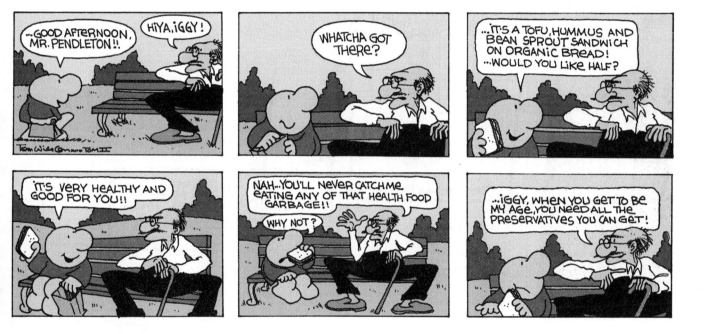

66

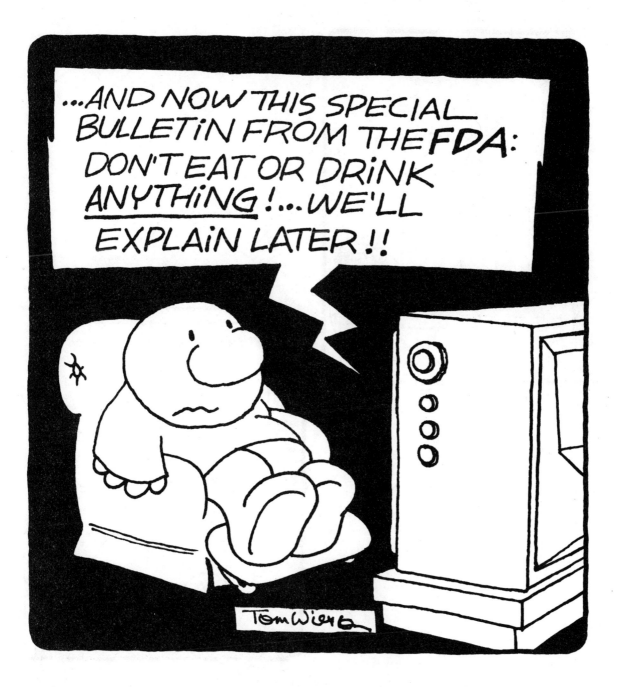

...WONDER WHAT'S OUT THERE IN THE GREAT BEYOND?...
...WHERE DOES IT ALL END?

111

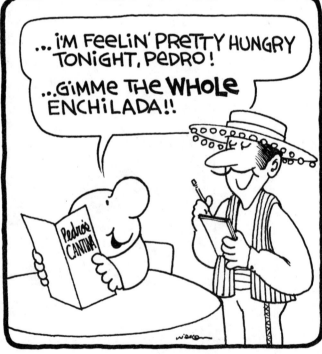

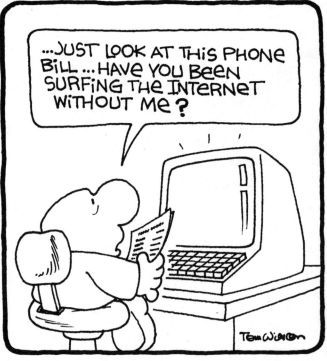